HOME COLLEGING

BECAUSE YOU HAVE NO CHOICE

LUMPKIN HOME COLLEGE

PATRICIA MARX and **SARAH PAYNE STUART**

WORKMAN PUBLISHING • NEW YORK

TO PETER WORKMAN

Copyright © 2014 by Patricia Marx and Sarah Payne Stuart

Portions of this book previously appeared in a different form in *The New Yorker*.

Library of Congress Cataloging-in-Publication Data is available.

ISBN 978-0-7611-5890-5

Cover design by Vaughn Andrews
Interior design by Lisa Hollander
Photo research by Michael DiMascio
Digital imaging by James T. Williamson
Original photography by Evan Sklar
Wardrobe styling by Ellen Silverstein

Additional photo credits appear on page 120

Workman books are available at special discounts when purchased in bulk for
premiums and sales promotions as well as for fund-raising or educational use.
Special editions or book excerpts can also be created to specification. For details,
contact the Special Sales Director at the address below, or send an email to
specialmarkets@workman.com.

Workman Publishing Co., Inc.
225 Varick Street
New York, NY 10014-4381
workman.com

WORKMAN is a registered trademark of Workman Publishing Co., Inc.

Printed in the United States of America

First printing May 2014

10 9 8 7 6 5 4 3 2 1

Lumpkin Home College and all characters appearing in this work are fictitious. Any
resemblance to real institutions or to persons, living or dead, is purely coincidental.
Ideas gleaned from this book are not applicable toward college credit, and study
habits described herein are not recommended. Do not try this at home unless your
child has made every other option impossible.

CONTENTS

WHY LUMPKIN?

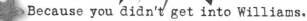 Because you didn't get into Williams.

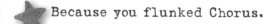 Because of that thing with the police.

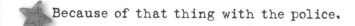 Because you flunked Chorus.

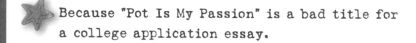 Because "Pot Is My Passion" is a bad title for a college application essay.

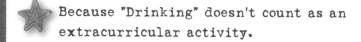 Because "Drinking" doesn't count as an extracurricular activity.

Because "none of the above" is not the correct answer to every question on the SATs.

Because you slept the whole way in the car when Daddy's friend who's a trustee at Middlebury drove you home from guitar camp.

Because you didn't listen to us when we told you to apply to a safety school.

Because you don't know the difference between *who* and *whom*.

 Because you took Ceramics instead of Physics.

 Because spray-painting "Skateboarding Is Not a Crime" on a railroad bridge doesn't count as community service.

 Because *To Kill a Mockingbird* is not about "bird abuse."

 Because you're not in an a capella group like Jason Jerome-Pike.

 Because you didn't write your Williams interviewer a two-page thank-you note like Jason Jerome-Pike.

 Because "just chilling" is not a varsity sport.

 Because you're a felon.

 Because $43,879.

 Because that doesn't include books.

 Because, honey, you have no choice.

*Making the Best of a Bad Situation

Welcome to
LUMPKIN
HOME COLLEGE

Bunch of Junk and Student Lounge

Admissions Office

The Quad

Situated on a sweeping quarter acre in a center-hall Colonial that could use some paint, Lumpkin Home College is a highly selective, not-so-liberal residential college with a rigorous admission policy if you are not a blood relative.

We accept students who:

a) Were wait-listed at the Atlas Air Conditioner Repair School,

b) Did not get into Williams College, and c) are named Bradley H. Lumpkin.

How Do I Know If Lumpkin Is Right for Me?

Are you an intellectual risk-taker who revels in pushing the boundaries of your comfort zone? A crusader out to change the world who believes indifference is the greatest crime of all? A lifetime learner and creative thinker ready to take ownership of his or her own education? Did you ever once in 17 years do your homework? Have you ever read a book? Do you know who the president of the United States is?

If you answered no to these questions—and to most questions—then you are just the student that Lumpkin is looking for. In fact, the only student Lumpkin is looking for.

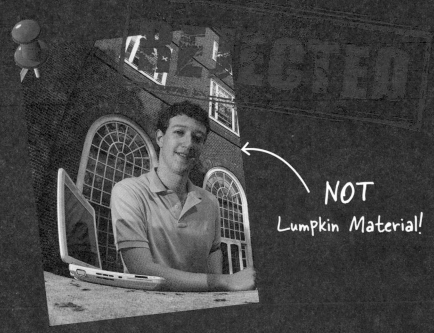

NOT
Lumpkin Material!

Cost Comparison of Home College vs. Sleep-Away College

Save a bundle

COMMUTING:
HOME COLLEGE:
$78.01
(includes gasoline
to weekly probation
meetings at annex
campus, Precinct 41)
VS.
**SLEEP-AWAY
COLLEGE: $2,356**
(includes buying a
ticket to Tulsa instead
of Tucson)

ENTERTAINMENT:
HOME COLLEGE: $0
(fun not allowed)
VS.
SLEEP-AWAY COLLEGE: $832,
not including hard liquor (add $200 for
University of Iowa; deduct $200 for Swarthmore)

LAUNDRY:
HOME COLLEGE: $0
VS.
SLEEP-AWAY COLLEGE: $873
(includes cost of shipping 25
pounds of dirty clothes home
every semester)

TOOTHPASTE:
HOME COLLEGE: $0
VS.
SLEEP-AWAY
COLLEGE: $0

TEXTBOOKS:
HOME COLLEGE: $0
("Isn't texting, like, free?")
VS.
SLEEP-AWAY COLLEGE: $250

THE LUMPKIN DIFFERENCE.

The student who is not Lumpkin material is easily recognizable by characteristics beyond his impressive ability to speak in sentences and look at his mother when she talks to him.

Jason Jerome-Pike

NOT LUMPKIN →

ATTITUDE-
Has confidence knowing he sent Williams interviewer a thank-you note.

GROOMING-
Wears clean shirt (which he ironed himself, Bradley).

SUPPLIES- Has already downloaded Williams freshman course syllabus to his iPad.

Bradley H. Lumpkin

LUMPKIN ↓ MATERIAL

The Lumpkin student is immediately identifiable by characteristics that set him apart from students who elect more traditional educational options. His focus is less on the outer world than the inner one; he believes resources not reachable from his bed are not worth reaching for.

ATTITUDE-Feels that if he was meant to go to college, one would be named for him. Surprise!

SUPPLIES-Believes "cannabis" entry from 1985 *Encyclopaedia Britannica* should be entire freshman curriculum.

GROOMING- Holds the world's record for longest round-the-clock wearing of the same unwashed jeans.

Admissions

O········ Looking Beyond the Numbers

Lumpkin does not rely solely on the standardized test results of an applicant who "loosened up" before the SAT by having a beer with Gabriel in the woods. Rather, our application review process is a holistic one, taking into account the whole of the Lumpkin home mortgage, with an emphasis on the balloon payment due in January. (See Financial Loans for Parents.)

O········ Late Decision

While many high-profile colleges continue to debate the fairness of Early Decision, Lumpkin Home College is fast becoming known for its signature Late Decision. "Lumpkin Late" is ideally suited to those students who forgot to mail the application fee to Skidmore College.

DID YOU KNOW? Home-college students make 3 percent of the annual income of graduates of the University of Idaho!

Application committee during review process

⭘ ·········· Interviews

Student interviews are required and will take place with our Admissions Associate, the applicant's little brother, Timmy, this Saturday night for approximately one to four hours, depending upon how many tequila shots Mommy and Daddy will need after attending the Teacher Appreciation Potluck Dinner at the elementary school.

Alumni interviews with Mommy, the Dean of Admissions, are also required (on a daily basis), even after a student is enrolled in Lumpkin Home College. Be prepared to answer the following questions: What is that smell in your room? How many times have we told you your roommate, Timmy, is not to be locked in the closet? Why is everything you do an attack on me?

Off-campus interview may also be required: Check with your attorney.

Interview Tips:
- ★ Wear clothing.
- ★ Eyes should be open.
- ★ Face the interviewer.

The interview gives applicants the opportunity to learn more about the college and share further information about themselves with the Admissions Committee.

**Lumpkin Home College
Personal Statement**

Lumpkin prides itself on close communication between the administration and the student. In that spirit, tell us something about yourself that your test scores, GPA, and the Incomplete in Gym simply cannot. Your essay is a wonderful opportunity to share your thoughts with the Admissions Committee and Dickie "ZZ" Fled, your Probation Officer.

CHOOSE ONE OF THE FOLLOWING TOPICS:

★ Why I love the generous gift certificate from Amazon I got *one year ago*, and how sorry I am that I did not send a thank-you sooner. (Please address this to Aunt Bunny and Uncle Morris.)

★ Why I didn't listen to my parents last summer when they said on more than one occasion that it would look good on my Carnegie Mellon application if I were a counselor at *Camp Global Relief for Juvenile Survivors of the Bosnian Civil War.*

★ Why I am not more like Jason Jerome-Pike. (No word limit.)

★ "I have no idea why that police cruiser is always parked outside." True or False? Elaborate.

★ When exactly I am planning to clean up that vomit in the powder room wastebasket.

★ John Donne's poem "At the Round Earth's Imagined Corners Blow" was written nearly 400 years ago, yet it speaks to us as directly and urgently as if we were receiving a confidence by text message. Examine this poem's relevance for us today. (No word limit.)

Bradley Lumpkin's Essay
for Williams College*

* Written 20 minutes before deadline by Dean Mommy Lumpkin

If you could hold any position in government, what would it be? Why?

If I could hold any position in government, I would be President. This seems a clear choice since the President is higher up than other politicians and would, arguably, have more power to effect real change. What would distinguish a person fortunate enough to be given this extraordinary opportunity-- and opportunities to become President do not come often in a person's life--is how he or she would use that power. This is where I come in.

As President, I would do two things right off the bat. The first thing I would do is appoint my mother to an important post, with a commensurate salary, designed specifically to suit her talents. Say . . . Secretary of the Arts and Life.

What many people probably do not know is that, as a child, my mother loved plunging her hands into the cool, mucous clay in art class and squirting it at people. She also has excellent secretarial skills. Her husband is kind of a dope.

As a fair annual salary for the position of Secretary of the Arts and Life, $200,000, or even maybe $220,000, pops into mind.

For too long, our government has been characterized by partisan fighting and divisiveness. We've grown sadly unaccustomed to the old, "antiquated" ideals of life, liberty, and the pursuit of happiness. We have, each of us, lost track of who we really are.

Therefore, we must ask ourselves, "Who are we?" This is a stimulating question.

Never, never quit. Instead, always go the distance. When you are pushing yourself to the limit time and time again, climbing that mountain or riding your stationary bike, depend on all your inner strength to pull you through. Love is all we need, except we also need to go the distance.

Part of the job requirement for the post of Secretary of the Arts and Life would be that the Secretary live in King of Prussia, Pennsylvania, and have an in-ground pool.

The second thing I would do as President is to introduce a bill or something.

About Lumpkin Home College

A LETTER FROM OUR PRESIDENT

Dear Incoming Freshman,

Welcome to Lumpkin Home College, the only higher education institution on Red Rambler Lane. Whether you are a returning student or are just beginning your journey at L.H.C.—or, as in the case of Bradley H. Lumpkin, both—you have enrolled at an exciting time! At the end of this year, we will be celebrating our first year of excellence. Plans are already kicking off for Lumpkin's Bicentennial, just 200 years away!

Lumpkin Home College, founded last Tuesday night after the police removed the handcuffs, is dedicated to instilling in Bradley H. Lumpkin an appreciation of staying out of jail. In addition to its mandatory work-study program, the college is known for its high faculty–student ratio, particularly if you count Grandma. The conveniently compact campus is located just minutes

From the desk of Florence Lumpkin

from a nail salon, an auto upholstery shop, and the Feigenberg family, where students who are no longer on probation can take their junior year abroad.

More great news! As a matriculating freshman, you have been assigned to live in the same dormitory as the faculty. You will be residing in the Lumpkin Unkempt Center, which you may recall as the room that overlooks the driveway, now known as the quad, and already contains your stuff and Timmy. Downstairs, you will find the cafeteria, where we make sure that your dining experience is about more than just leftovers: It's about cleanup, too. New student, please take note: Lumpkin still does not have a liquor license. The cabinet in Marvin Feigenberg's study is reserved solely for visiting professors in need of refreshment.

At Lumpkin Home College, we recognize that education goes beyond intellectual discourse. Each weekend, we'll hop in the Explorer and head out to the turnpike. Here,

From the desk of Florence Lumpkin

the underclassman can fulfill his court-ordered Phys. Ed. requirement by picking up litter along exits 37 to 39. And it's not for nothing that our team mascots are the Mighty Fighting Attorneys of Arffa, Sheanshang & Wadia. This year, we're hoping to trounce the New Jersey State of Appeals. Go Lumpkin Attorneys!

Lumpkin Home College is not all fun and games, however. Aside from Yale, L.H.C. is the only college in America where first-year students gather to wet mop Grandma's room every Thursday, which is the least you can do after what you did to her credit rating.

What kind of a school is this? Unlike at other universities, learning at Lumpkin does not just take place in traditional classrooms. Here, classes are conducted in the living room, the kitchen, the garage, even in the car, as the faculty and student journey together on field trips to watch Timmy in a Little League game or take our college mascot, Sarge, to the vet for deworming. At Lumpkin, education is a 24/7 adventure.

From the desk of Florence Lumpkin

We offer courses not only during the day but in the evening, on the weekends, even on Christmas, when the entire college is treated to the annual lecture by Uncle Mitch on how he could have been a rock star if he'd stuck with the mandolin.

We hope you will not think of Lumpkin as your home away from home, because it isn't. It's an institution.

Finally, I would like to mention that for many parents, watching a son or daughter leave for school is an emotional time. I wish I could say the same.

Sincerely,

~~Mommy~~

President Mrs. Lumpkin

U.S. World & COLLEGE RANKINGS News Report

feature	ranking
Faculty–Student Ratio	#1
Best Lighting of Patio	#1
Best Homemade Lemon Squares	#3
Least Tolerant Windowsill Marijuana-Growing Policy	#1
Unhappiest Students	#1
Strictest Bedtime Policy	#1
You Call This a Social Life?	#2
Diverse Student Body	#392
Financial Aid	#2
Wall-to-Wall Carpeting	#1
Town–Gown Relations (Best Rapport with Locksmith)	#2
Greenest Snacks	#6
Craziest Uncle	#1
Most Lavish Mother's Day Celebration	#1
Best Board Game Night	#7
Most Comprehensive Babysitting Services	#2
Worst Radio Reception in Bathroom	#12
Lots of Toothpaste	#4
Quietest Basement Dehumidifier	#14
Most Reasonably Priced Laundry Facility	#13
Best Santana and Karen Carpenter Mixtape Collection	#1
Worst Technical Support Staff	#1

Lumpkin Home College has an illustrious history, reaching back many minutes to a heritage seldom seen in a college established in lieu of jail time. As president and founder, it is hard to remember a past when there was no Lumpkin Home College without weeping uncontrollably. And yet there are quiet moments when I and Lumpkin's Comptroller and Dean of Thankless Chores, Daddy, travel down memory lane to the day before yesterday: when a certain party was still going to get rid of his junk in the rumpus room that was slated to become his mother's office/guest room/Grandma's Inner-Child Dance Studio; when a bright future beckoned of Saturday nights when President Mrs. Lumpkin and Comptroller Mr. Lumpkin might pull out of the driveway for a quick movie without a hundred teenagers' cars pulling in; when the milk carton wasn't put back in the fridge with a single drop left in it; when the fact that Yale was Gina Henderson's daughter's safety school might one day be as expunged from our minds as the memory of our own criminal teenage activities.

Time Line of History of Lumpkin Home College

2:03 AM

2:04 AM

2:03 a.m. Last Night Mommy and Daddy sleeping soundly.

2:03 a.m. Daddy's cell rings for a full minute (Adele's "Someone Like You"); Daddy curses looking for phone, stubs toe; Sarge barks and claws new chenille bedspread.

2:04 a.m. Officer Hanley wonders if Daddy can answer the question "Where is your son?"

2:04 a.m. Daddy is informed that "sleeping in the next room because he has church in the morning" is the incorrect answer. Sarge, still barking, tries to hump Daddy.

DID YOU KNOW? In Middle English, the word for "home college" is *homecollege*!

2:05 AM

2:08 AM

2:05 a.m. Mommy grabs phone and feigns surprise to learn that son has lied, giving officer his name as "Jason Jerome-Pike" (and was betrayed by library card).

2:05 a.m. "My son would *never* have a library card on his person!" Mommy retorts indignantly, while admitting that paying a homeless man to buy him vodka and then partying with him across the street from a police station is more in realm of son's potential.

2:05 a.m. Sarge, still excited, pees on that place on the carpet.

2:06 a.m. In the bathroom, Mommy loses two contact lenses in succession.

2:08 a.m. Daddy and Mommy blame each other for everything. Lumpkin Home College is founded in car on way to Precinct 41.

COMMITMENT TO DIVERSITY

Since its founding, Lumpkin Home College has dedicated itself to offering all female individuals, regardless of race, ethnicity, or gender, the opportunity to date Bradley H. Lumpkin, provided they are not Audrey Fish. It does not care if your blood type is A, B, AB, or O, whether you are left-handed or right-handed, or what color your iPad case is. L.H.C. is more concerned with what you can provide for Bradley H. Lumpkin, in terms of his intellectual development and also in terms of jobs and money after he graduates.

TYPES OF GIRLFRIENDS LUMPKIN HOME COLLEGE DOES NOT DISCRIMINATE AGAINST:

Charlotte $$$—Daughter of Mr. and Mrs. $$$. Mrs. $$$ is the CEO and Chair of the $$$ Foundation, an organization that gives out money of all denominations to undeserving college graduates. Mr. $$$ heads the Nepotism Employment Agency.

Candy Kane—Babysitter for Bradley H. Lumpkin's roommate. Loves to clean up. Knows how to say please and thank you in 27 languages. Hobbies include loading the dishwasher, folding, and drinking milk. Knows how to read. If she were Bradley's girlfriend, Lumpkin Home College would save $9 an hour.

Meg Yih—Accepted to every Ivy League college and plans to attend all of them. She will double-major in Cancer Curing at Harvard and Comparative History of Everything at Princeton. Yale has offered her a deanship. She has accepted a scholarship to run track for all the Division One teams (men's and women's). In her spare time, she enjoys basket-weaving.

TYPES OF GIRLFRIENDS LUMPKIN HOME COLLEGE DOES DISCRIMINATE AGAINST:

5'10"
5'8"
5'6"
5'4"
5'2"
5'0"
4'10"
4'8"
4'6"
4'4"
4'2"
4'4"

POLICE DEPARTMENT
MUGSHOT

State Police
Fingerprint Record

Right Hand

Index Finger

Middle Finger

Ring Fing

Left Hand

Pinky Finger

Ring Finger

Middle Finger

Inde

INVEST

UNWANTED
AUDREY FISH

AIDING AND ABETTING • ARSON • ASSAULT • BATTERY • BRIBERY • BURGLARY • CHILD ABANDONMENT • CHILD ABUSE • CHILD PORNOGRAPHY • COMPUTER CRIME • CONSPIRACY • CREDIT AND DEBIT CARD FRAUD • CRIMINAL CONTEMPT OF COURT • CYBERBULLYING • DISORDERLY CONDUCT • DISTURBING THE PEACE • DOMESTIC VIOLENCE • DRUG MANUFACTURING AND CULTIVATION • DRUG POSSESSION • DRUG TRAFFICKING AND DISTRIBUTION • DUI • EMBEZZLEMENT • EXTORTION • FORGERY • HARASSMENT • HATE CRIMES • HOMICIDE • IDENTITY THEFT • INDECENT EXPOSURE • INSURANCE FRAUD • KIDNAPPING • LARCENY • MANSLAUGHTER (INVOLUNTARY AND VOLUNTARY) • MONEY LAUNDERING • MURDER (FIRST- AND SECOND-DEGREE) • OPEN CONTAINER LAW VIOLATION • PERJURY • POSSESSION OF MEDICAL MARIJUANA • PROBATION VIOLATION • PROSTITUTION • PUBLIC INTOXICATION • PYRAMID SCHEMES • RACKETEERING • RAPE • RICO • ROBBERY • SECURITIES FRAUD • SEXUAL ASSAULT • SHOPLIFTING • SOLICITATION • STALKING • STATUTORY RAPE • TAX EVASION • TELEMARKETING FRAUD • THEFT • VANDALISM • WHITE-COLLAR CRIMES • WIRE FRAUD

2.5 MILLION–3000 B.C. STONE AGE: Original "Home School of Rock."

2036 B.C.: The True or False test perfected. Had hitherto been the False or False test. Millions of students flunk.

8000 B.C.: Beginning of agriculture. First time Brussels sprouts uneaten in a school lunch satchel.

3100 B.C.: Oldest known example of student being treated for nosebleed by school nurse.

776 B.C.: In Greece, gym class renamed Olympics. Twenty-seven girls bring in notes from home saying they have their periods and can't participate.

HOME EDUCATION

1 2 3

20,000 B.C.: First arts and crafts project.

5000 B.C.: Discovery of fire and school bake sales.

431 B.C.: Single stay-at-home mom Medea home-schools her two children after their deadbeat dad, Jason, takes off. Tragedy ensues.

1347: Bubonic plague spreads through Europe. Sex-education programs in the home are blamed.

3000 B.C.: Sumerians invent written language. First term paper extension granted.

1437: Hundred Years' War ends. Study reveals 93 percent of students cannot figure out when the war began.

1700s: Age of Enlightenment. Does not apply to those under 18.

1860–1865: Civil War in America. In some homes, sisters cheered against sisters.

1454: Printing press invented. Millions of children across Europe are given the opportunity not to read.

1776: Declaration of Independence. Student body of Winslow Home College gets plastered in the pursuit of happiness and wakes up the next morning in the bed of a Tory wench.

1928: Penicillin accidentally invented when student of Lavoisier Home College tries to smoke mold spores and discovers they cure bacterial infections.

THROUGH THE AGES 16 17

1492: Columbus sails to Hispaniola. Students flock there next year for spring break.

1837: Invention of the telegraph. First time youngsters neglect studies in order to tap short messages to their friends.

1930s: The Great Depression sinks the country. Bad student poetry is at an all-time high.

How r u?

1637: Analytic Geometry created. Incites first student protest movement.

1964: Flipper, first home-schooled dolphin, gets his own TV show.

1689: English Bill of Rights signed. Home-school dress codes relaxed for Protestants.

2009: Home-colleged sophomore Penny Jackson is the first person to map the human genome. Results not valid when it was discovered she cheated by using a GPS.

LUMPKIN LORE

MISSION STATEMENT:
WE'RE JUST TRYING TO MAKE THE
BEST OF A BAD SITUATION

**LUMPKIN
MOTTO:**

NOSTRI PUERUM
("OUR BOY")

Lumpkin Mascot
Sarge, Family Pet

Not Leaving on a Jet Plane

by Bradley H. Lumpkin

All my bags aren't packed, I'm fated to stay,
I'm standing here right by the door,
I'd hoped to pick the lock then say good-bye.
But the latch is broken, it's [f***ing] jammed,
The parents woke up, now I'm really damned.
Already I'm so grounded I could cry.

So save me and pray for me,
Tell my mom she's history.
Call someone and tell them let me go,
'Cause I'm trapped here in this hellhole.
Don't know when I can take a stroll.
Oh babe, I want to go.

I've so many friends, they're leaving town,
So many friends, they're off to Brown.
I tell you now, high school's looking good.
Emory, Penn, Cornell, and NYU,
Colby, Duke, UConn, Deep Springs, Wash U.
Oh, take me now, I'll wear your camo hood.

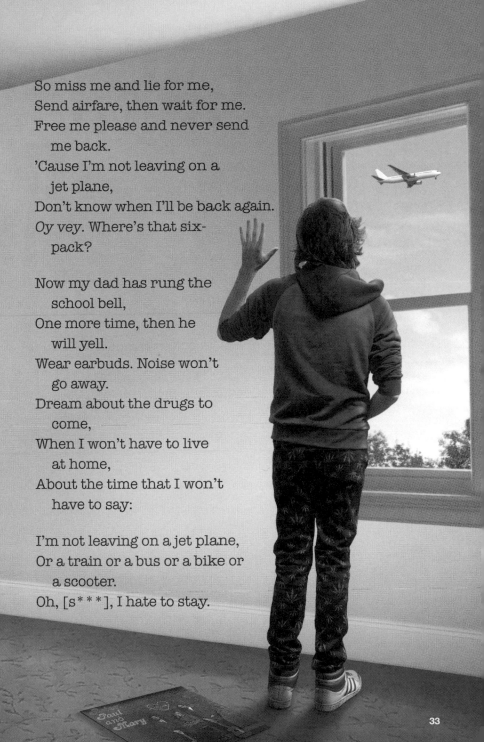

So miss me and lie for me,
Send airfare, then wait for me.
Free me please and never send
    me back.
'Cause I'm not leaving on a
    jet plane,
Don't know when I'll be back again.
Oy vey. Where's that six-
    pack?

Now my dad has rung the
    school bell,
One more time, then he
    will yell.
Wear earbuds. Noise won't
    go away.
Dream about the drugs to
    come,
When I won't have to live
    at home,
About the time that I won't
    have to say:

I'm not leaving on a jet plane,
Or a train or a bus or a bike or
    a scooter.
Oh, [s***], I hate to stay.

33

FACULTY AND STAFF

Florence "Mommy" Lumpkin, President. Also: Dean of Student; Eugene McCarthy Professor of Lost Dreams Studies; Professor of Fruitless Regret; Chair of the Department of Wishing and Housing; Chair of the Department of Housekeeping; Chair of the Animal Care Committee

President Mrs. Lumpkin is the author of a wide variety of college application essays, including "How My Academic Achievements in High School Have Informed and Transformed My Personal Goals by Bradley H. Lumpkin," awarded Best

"I need to know where you're going, who you're going with, and the phone numbers of everyone's parents."

Fiction of the Year by Lumpkin faculty and friends. Arriving on campus, pregnant with hope and Lumpkin's current matriculant, she has had 18 years' experience locating the beginning of the ClingWrap. President Mrs. Lumpkin also retains the distinction of being the only human at Lumpkin who has ever fed the dog. Affectionately called Mommy by the entire student body (as well as the student body's

roommate, Timmy), our president is known for her unrealistic optimism, overbearing concern, and Tuna Taco Surprise. She received her master's degree in Revisionist History from ~~DegreeFactory.com~~ Columbia University.

ASPIRATIONS: To turn back the clock to any time before Bradley's suspension from middle school for sexual harassment.

"Did anyone see the mayonnaise?"

Before becoming our chief financial officer, Ron served as Scout leader, carpool driver, grill master, and nap taker. A modern dad, he attended Lamaze class with President Mrs. Lumpkin and used the word *vagina* in conversation 213 times the week following Bradley's birth.

Eighteen years later, it was Ron who had the business acumen to realize that funding a college could actually be a money-saver!

As overseer of the school endowment, he has cut costs by not allowing students to have a car and refinancing the campus. In his spare time, Ron runs the Lumpkin Bubble Wrap Company, where Bradley was an unpaid intern until he was let go for organizing a pay strike among the factory employees. Comptroller Mr. Lumpkin's hobbies include waterboarding.

ASPIRATION: To find the mustard in the refrigerator.

NAP AND OFFICE HOURS: Monday–Friday: after 7 p.m.; Saturday and Sunday: all day.

"Like it or Lumpkin."

"I'll be 39 next July."

Gramz _____ (fill in with name of current husband), Jocelyn Wildenstein Professor of Cosmetic Surgery. Also: Chair of the Gossip, Hearsay, and Calumny Department; Professor of Freeloading Studies

Gramz has been a visiting professor at Lumpkin since September when she was dumped by her fifth husband and came to live in the student lounge. An advocate of single-sex education (provided the sex is male), Gramz has single-handedly mounted a campaign to expand college enrollment by offering scholarships to eligible older men. This semester, Gramz will be teaching a class in computer dating. The class will be held in the cafeteria, where Gramz promises to fix anyone in pants one of her famous Lumpkin vodka tonics.

ASPIRATION: To meet Starsky (but will settle for Hutch).

"Just because you're the president doesn't mean you aren't my daughter, so stop telling me what's appropriate behavior for a 73-year-old."

"It's not fair!"

Bradley's seven-year-old roommate, Timmy the Tattletale, has been a member of the Lumpkin Home College community his whole life. At the request of his parents, Timmy sometimes wears a wire and a suit of armor. While at Lumpkin, Timothy has distinguished himself by being the only human who is able to turn the new TV both on *and* off, and his workshop "TV Made Simple" is a perennial favorite at Lumpkin. Be sure to catch Timmy next semester in the college's production of *Once Upon a Mattress*, in which he plays the mattress.

"Help!"

ASPIRATION: That Bradley will move to Afghanistan.

"Slurp."

After receiving his doctorate in bad behavioral sciences from the ASPCA, Sarge was adopted as the Lumpkin Home College mascot and the director of garbage-regurgitation, with a specialty in chicken carcasses. His interests include the cigarettes in Bradley's backpack, wrapped Christmas presents, and tonight's dinner. As the only dog in the world that actually "ate the homework," Sarge has digested information in topics ranging from the Pythagorean theorem to Spanish verbs. When he is not sleeping, Sarge enjoys shedding and long drives in the car.

ASPIRATION: To have puppies with the bitch next door.

"Please sign here."

Jeff, who originally hails from FedEx, adds a lot to everyday life at Lumpkin, especially in paper goods. Every holiday season, President Mrs. Lumpkin and Comptroller Mr. Lumpkin hold a seminar on the topic of how much to tip UPS Jeff.

ASPIRATION: To deliver a package to himself.

A graduate of Skalen Home College in 2002, Sis is a shining example of how far you can go without a degree from a so-called real college. Even if you don't know how to read!

ASPIRATION: "Aspirin is in aisle three."

"If you give me, like, a $20 bill for, like, a $1 item, I'll give you, like, three fives and four dollars. We're out of tens."

Mrs. Jiffy "I'm Blessed" Jerome-Pike, Mother of Jason Jerome-Pike. Also: Uninvited Guest Lecturer; President of the Persona Non Grata Society

"What were Bradley's board scores again?"

Mother of five children accepted at Ivy League colleges before they reached middle school, Jiffy Jerome-Pike brings to Lumpkin a certain je ne sais quoi, as well as a court order to stay at least 100 yards away from President Mrs. Lumpkin, or President Mrs. Lumpkin "will not be responsible for her actions."

Author of *Guess Who's Coming for Dinner?*

ASPIRATION: That Bradley never date any of her children.

A firm believer that life is rigged anyway, self-appointed

"My sister, her son never gone to college, and they give him a suit when he got out of prison, never been worn."

Adjunct Professor Dawna is a frequent commentator on the Lumpkin Home College experience, without ever having stepped beyond the deli counter except (possibly) to stamp out her cigarette. Dawna's renowned lecture, "Best Thing That Ever Happened to Bradley H. Lumpkin Was Not Getting into College," has been regaling people in the cold cuts line since Comptroller Mr. Lumpkin received the Instagram of Bradley's Atlas Air Conditioner Repair School wait-list letter while waiting for his macaroni salad, extra mayo.

ASPIRATION: To no longer have to pretend she isn't still using the knife she just dropped on the floor for the 100th time.

"How about checking this time before you turn on the garbage disposal."

Perky LeBron Lumpkin I, II, III, IV, Adjunct Professor of Terminal Studies. Also: Coach, Varsity Basketball; Timmy's Turtle(s)

Known for his steadily softening shell and enviable moves on the turtle pong table, Perky (and his replacements) brings a unique combo of old-fashioned fun and impending doom to the Lumpkin campus. The student learns the valuable lesson that if Timmy ever finds out that Perky is not the original Perky, the student body's car privileges will be revoked permanently.

Author of *Where Have All the Turtles Gone?*; *As I Lay Softening*; *Next Time, Get a Newt.*

ASPIRATION: To be fed.

YO! YO! YO! HAPPY HOLIDAYS

THOREAU UNPLUGGED

CASE LAW: SARGE VS. A NEW FRENCH DOOR FOR THE KITCHEN

THE LITERATURE OF THE ICE MAKER

ENGLISH AS A VANISHING LANGUAGE

REMEDIAL HISTORY 000

IT'S ABOUT TIME: AN INTRODUCTION TO THE CLOCK

INTRODUCTION TO ABNORMAL PSYCHOLOGY

SEX ED, ADVANCED

INTRODUCTION TO ABNORMAL PSYCHOLOGY

MUSIC UN-APPRECIATION

COURSE CATALOG

HOW TO MARRY A MILLIONAIRE (OR AT LEAST A THOUSANDAIRE)

GEOGRAPHY 100: HOW TO GET HOME WITHOUT A GPS

HISTORY OF MODERN SLAVERY

MARY MAGDALENE: SAINT OR AUDREY FISH?

THE PERFECT STORM (WINDOW)

MICROWAVE THEORY

LAUNDRY 101

Does Lumpkin have academics?

You bet.

Among the classes we are proud to offer are the following:

THINGS AIN'T WHAT THEY USED TO BE: A Dialectic of Mother–Son Relationships

In this course, we'll explore various forms of government from anarchy to Bradocracy. Is despotism really so terrible? You might be surprised by the answer. Prerequisite: Apology Workshop.

ARCHAEOLOGY 206

Includes a field trip to Bradley H. Lumpkin's bed, where we will excavate for pizza crusts and coinage, as well as cell phones dating back to the early Paleo-iPhone era. Starts today.

Why would someone bury his little brother under a snowdrift, especially when you know Timmy worships you? Is it normal to sell your parents' car on eBay without their knowledge? These are some of the questions we'll analyze in this freshman tutorial. Meets once a week on Dr. Finkelstein's couch.

APPLIED MATHEMATICS

Focuses on solving real-life problems, such as: "If Bradley claims he invited 10 friends to his party but more than 200 youngsters show up, how much damage

will result, both in terms of dollars and euros, since two of the girls are French?" We'll also calculate whether the Lumpkins can afford to repair the roof after they've paid off their mortgage with the funds they would have remitted to Mountain Dew University if Bradley had completed his application in time. Meets Saturday nights, 7 p.m. to midnight.

THE FUNDAMENTALS OF ART APPRECIATION

A survey course of early antiquities, especially the broken one in the living room.

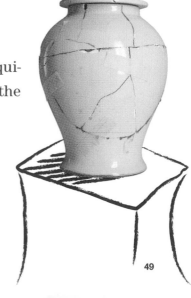

ENGLISH AS A VANISHING LANGUAGE

A weeklong intensive seminar in which we will discuss what is wrong with the sentence: "Some dude's cousin from Brooklyn must of put that bag of weed there." Prerequisite: Pencil.

SUPER-CRITICAL THINKING

A consideration of the quandary, "Why the heck was Bradley H. Lumpkin caught in flagrante delicto with Audrey Fish who's clearly such an airhead?" Required Reading: Text messages between Audrey Fish and Bradley Lumpkin. Prerequisite: Gender Politics and Audrey Fish 202.

THEATER II: CHARACTER MASK

How to deliver scripted lines for a court appearance with a remorse that moves. Extra-credit project: Student masters pronouncing, "Not guilty, Your Honor" with a sweep of integrity and the force necessary to convince.

OUR SUSTAINABLE EARTH

If you mix the garbage with the recyclables, they won't take it.

HOW TO MARRY A MILLIONAIRE
(or at Least a Thousandaire)

Taught by Visiting Professor Gramz, this class meets Monday–Friday between husbands. Bad advice is liberally dispensed and Gramz's sordid dating experiences raked over relentlessly until the student grasps the meaning of the maxim "Those who can, drink." Prerequisite: Wine coolers.

Sis Skalen, Chair of the Department of Economics and 7-Eleven Checkout Wiz, explains in layman terms the secrets of success in the global economy. Subjects include: the overlooked art of finger counting; invented spelling (and Sis's specialty, invented math); nap-time at the register; why saying "Use words, not fists" doesn't really work if the guy has a gun.

GAME THEORY

An endless lecture concerning the theories about why video games are not allowed at Lumpkin Home College.

DID YOU KNOW? Most fish swim in schools, but only halibut swim in home colleges!

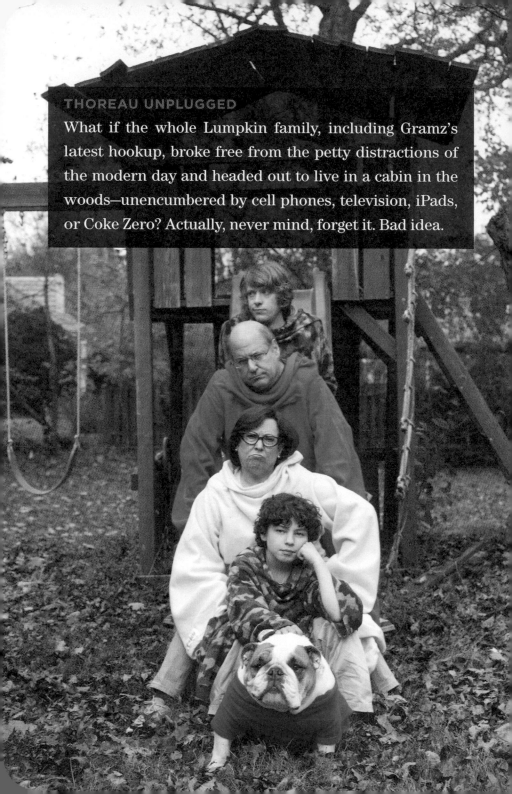

THOREAU UNPLUGGED
What if the whole Lumpkin family, including Gramz's latest hookup, broke free from the petty distractions of the modern day and headed out to live in a cabin in the woods—unencumbered by cell phones, television, iPads, or Coke Zero? Actually, never mind, forget it. Bad idea.

Questions addressed include:

Is Alaska in Canada?

Is the chief product of England rain?

Do Malaysians live in Malaria?

Is the Gaza Strip located in the red-light district?

Who killed the Dead Sea?

Is the Tropic of Cancer a tanning salon?

Does the Devil live in the Netherlands?

Can you measure the area of the Bermuda Triangle with a protractor or do you need an Equator?

How many singers make up an archipelago?

Why do they say "east" and "west" instead of "left" and "right"?

Where is the south?

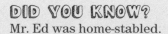

DID YOU KNOW?
Mr. Ed was home-stabled.

The ungraspable concept of who would eat a one-pound block of Parmesan cheese while it was still frozen unless they were stoned is further explored. Prerequisite: Refrigerator 101: Who Eats an Entire Cheesecake While It's Still Hot?

HOPE SPRINGS ETERNAL: Remedial Philosophy 000

Adjunct Professor Dawna from the deli counter ponders the following philosophical quandaries: What if some person on the phone you've never heard of tells you you've won a Grand Cherokee Jeep 2016 in a contest you never entered and all you have to do is send $256 to cover shipping, and you can't put your hand on that kind of money—will a bank lend it to you? What about the fact that you can lose 20 pounds a week by eating ice cream sandwiches in bed, something to do with digesting cold stuff lying down? Also, defining your brows takes 10 years off a person's life. It's been proven.

LOST IN TRANSLATION 200: English for Seniors

Associate Professor Timmy Lumpkin, Chair of the Department of Nonexistent Foreign Languages, will try to explain yet again the meaning of "Windows All Downloader," "Click Free PDF," and "Zulu Malware" to members of the senior faculty, who were sorry they asked.

The dual-tempered $349 French door that President Mrs. Lumpkin has wanted ever since she can remember and which would transform Lumpkin Home College kitchen by bringing in the outdoors as well as much-needed light, and which would allow the person who does virtually all the cooking for the university to go on living—is weighed against the cost of putting 12-year-old Sarge under general anesthesia to clean his teeth (and extract six dead ones). Lumpkin's martyred president finds in favor of Sarge but draws the line at putting Timmy's turtle, Perky LeBron Lumpkin III, on an IV because the vet says he's dehydrated.

THE PERFECT STORM (WINDOW)

Professor Daddy Lumpkin, Chancellor of the Exterior, explains in mind-numbing detail the numerous pluses and minuses of a seemingly endless, and endlessly similar, variety of storm windows he can't afford this year anyway. Class repeats every Saturday until the end of time.

IT'S ABOUT TIME:
An Introduction to the Clock

Did you know that it is possible to tell the time without turning on your cell phone? In this workshop, we will practice how to do this and discuss what it means to get somewhere "on time." We will discover how Einstein was wrong about time being relative and we will also learn the difference between real time and basketball and football time. Classes begin every morning when the big hand is on the "6" and the little hand is on the "8." If you are late, a concept that will be covered in classroom discussion, you will have to "do time."

LOGIC AND LOGISTICS 202

Taught by Comptroller Mr. Lumpkin, the eternal answer "Because I said so" is examined and found to be sufficient.

NATURE OR NURTURE?

Taught in tandem by our favorite faculty couple, Daddy and Mommy Lumpkin, each professor holds the other's family responsible for the current situation.

NOSTALGIA 101

The Days of Wine and Roses are remembered (or wine, anyway), when Bradley was still in elementary school and didn't know what a "Daddy drink" or "Mommy drink" was and the Lumpkin senior faculty could drink in peace. Extra credit awarded for cessation of the refrain "But you and Daddy drank at my age, and you *drove*."

A quick nip before the children grow up and figure out it's not orange juice?

A poetic cri de coeur by Professor Perky LeBron Lumpkin IV (Timmy's current turtle). Final Exam: Midnight burial in the garden, day to be announced.

PHYSICS 10,000,001

How the delicate, hand-painted Olde English butter dish—which President Mrs. Lumpkin bought with the per diem she earned before being excused from jury duty because her son might be a felon—ended up in a zillion pieces in a bottom desk drawer without anyone touching it is a wonder awaiting explanation by modern science. Registration fee: $49.99.

ADVANCED ETHICS 407

Taught by Comptroller/Chauffeur Mr. Lumpkin while driving in that place around Hartford where 40 is the speed limit but everyone drives 60, the student learns that while two wrongs do not make a right, a million wrongs do.

DID YOU KNOW? In Alsace-Lorraine, children teach their parents, and not vice versa!

MAGIC REALISM

This class will explore the possibility that, with a bridge loan, the campus could relocate to 1312 Barrowdale Road before that dormitory is purchased by another home college. The class, which involves numerous hopeful field trips to Barrowdale Road, is taught by Professor Mommy Lumpkin, Chair of the Department of Wishing and Housing.

DUMB AND DUMBER 401

If a certain leader in the field of higher education can't find her contacts case and puts her lenses in two paper cups and leaves them carefully out of the way on a shelf in a bathroom she shares with another leader in said field (to whom she is currently, if not irrevocably, married) and that other person fills both cups with water and drinks down both contact lenses, which innovator in the field of education is stupider? Enrollment closed to student.

Remember how President Mrs. Lumpkin told the student that even if he did a bad thing it didn't mean that he wasn't a good person? That she didn't want him to be perfect? That, in her eyes, he was perfect just the way he was? That there was not only an Easter Bunny, but a Valentine Bunny? You guessed it.

POLITICAL HISTORY 001: The Nazis and the Big Lie

An extremely cumbersome analogy is made between the vast fictions of the Nazi propaganda machine and Uncle Morris's bold-faced lies about how long it took him this year to get from his jazzy condo in Nashua, New Hampshire, to the Lumpkins' house in King of Prussia, Pennsylvania. Course offering (and Uncle Morris) limited to Thanksgiving and Christmas.

MUSIC UN-APPRECIATION 010

Class discussion will revolve around why you can't bring your iPhone to church, why that racket your band makes does not fit the definition of "music," and why the faculty always wears earplugs on campus, except for Professor Gramz, who has a thing for your drummer and is also deaf. Come to class prepared to listen to the sounds of silence.

REVISIONIST HISTORY 101

What if the American Revolution had never happened? What if there had never been any wars ever? If you could rewrite the history books, what would you write? This course, taught by President Mrs. Lumpkin, Professor of Fruitless Regret, asks the following provocative questions: What if we'd bought the colonial on Beech Court Drive instead of this one? What if I'd made Bradley join the Cub Scouts? What if I'd been thin in college instead of fat?

REMEDIAL HISTORY 000

Is it possible to erase the past? Professor Daddy Lumpkin proves that it is actually possible to take an old three-hour videotape, not notice it is boldly marked "Bradley and baby Timmy at Disneyland," and blithely use it to tape all 12 episodes of the E! celebrity show *Taradise*, thus deleting the most wonderful week, possibly ever, from his family's life.

SKATEBOARDING IS A CRIME...
and So Is Clicking on a Photo File on Daddy's Computer Labeled "Stoned in L.A."

First of all, that was really long ago, before Professors Mommy and Daddy Lumpkin were even married, and nobody wore bras back then, and the brownies looked like regular brownies, and now I think of it, we were just pretending to be stoned for the picture, and what's wrong with having a little fun, anyway, and what were you doing on Professor Daddy Lumpkin's laptop in the first place?

SEX EDUCATION, ADVANCED

A dialogue about, um, you know. We will dispense information about some stuff, and teach the student how to prevent things and avoid certain unnamed persons. Or maybe we will just go out to brunch. Not a hands-on approach. Do not try this at home.

APPLIED CHEMISTRY 203

A refresher course for students who cannot grasp, no matter how many times they've been lectured, that leaving a carton of milk under your bed for several weeks turns it green and catalyzes an unpleasant reaction on the face of Professor Mommy Lumpkin, director of the laboratory in the kitchen. We will also show how returning an empty container of ice cream to the freezer disproves the theory of spontaneous generation.

DID YOU KNOW? Clarence Darrow was home law-schooled!

PHYSICAL EDUCATION

This semester we will focus on getting up before 3 p.m.

DID YOU KNOW? The poet Emily Dickinson attended home college in her bed!

LAUNDRY 101: Pro and Con

A cost analysis is done by Professor Mommy Lumpkin, Chair of the Department of Housekeeping, on whether it's worth having the student throw his dirty pants in the washer unassisted if Daddy's uninsured smartphone is in a pocket.

STRING THEORY

Hey, what moron left dental floss on the stairs? This class will not be repeated.

MICROWAVE THEORY

A panel discussion open to all in which professors and student defend their various microwave philosophies. Comptroller Mr. Lumpkin unveils the revolutionary concept that opening the microwave four seconds before it says READY will save you four seconds. Student Bradley H. Lumpkin fires back with the non sequitur "We should sue the microwave people because they should of said not to nuke a potato 60 minutes with a fork in it." Gramz reminds the class that everyone knows microwaves give you cancer. Professor Mommy Lumpkin, Chair of the Department of Housekeeping, moderates without mercy.

THE LITERATURE OF THE ICE MAKER 101–2000

Required reading for entering freshman—as well as the literatures of the Bosch dishwasher, the air-conditioner unit we got on eBay that's all in Chinese, that stupid remote control device Uncle Morris gave us for the television so that now the TV doesn't go below channel 8000, and the "easy assembly" hanging medicine cabinet Gramz bought that isn't even real wood.

BIOGRAPHY 303 (FORMERLY GOSSIP 27)

In this seminar, held every morning at the breakfast table, Visiting Professor Gramz, Chair of the Gossip, Hearsay, and Calumny Department, will analyze the obituaries in the daily *King of Prussia Gazette*. Topics include: Is the deceased survived by an eligible man?

CAN VOMIT BE DISTINGUISHED BY SMELL? 201

Who threw up in Mommy's purse late Saturday night (and don't say Jason Jerome-Pike, who is building houses in India all week)? Can dog vomit be distinguished from human vomit? "I dunno, I must of got the flu" is set to music and performed as an interpretive dance by Audrey Fish.

DID YOU KNOW? At Goodenlach Home College in Switzerland, you can major in yodeling!

> <

Professor (and calorie-aficionado) Daddy Lumpkin demonstrates how dotting out a small circle in the center of a cherry pie with a knife and then quickly gobbling down all the rest straight from the pan with no one looking means you didn't technically eat a piece of pie. Visiting Professor (and eternal learner) Gramz proves empirically how substituting Burgundy wine for milk in French toast renders the sun-over-the-yardarm restriction moot.

In this class we will learn how to make art out of illegal objects.

AN AMERICAN TRAGEDY

Theodore Dreiser's classic tragedy is but a romp in the park compared to this searing saga of an American boy and his American dog (who wished only *for* a romp in the park). Sarge Lumpkin, Professor of Urology and Carpet Sciences, reminds us we need look no further than his own backyard to find canine rights being violated on a regular basis: Bradley passing out Saturday nights before letting Sarge out; Comptroller Mr. Lumpkin in his sleep kicking Sarge to the bottom of the bed; Timmy dressing Sarge in Supergirl costume; Gramz slobbering over Sarge after another romantic disappointment; even the light of Sarge's life, President Mrs. Lumpkin, more than once pouring the bacon grease in the trash instead of over Sarge's bowl of boring dry dog food. Required reading: *You Would Drink Out of the Toilet, Too, If the Water in Your Water Dish Was Four Days Old; Sarge the Obscure; You Can Spray Anything You Want on That Spot on the Rug, I'm Still Going to Pee on It.*

MARY MAGDALENE: Saint or Audrey Fish?

Courageous and loyal, Mary Magdalene is described in the Christian gospels as standing by after all but one of the male apostles had fled the scene of the crucifixion. Yet for centuries, Mary Magdalene was conflated with another Mary in the Bible, a prostitute. Were the Christian authorities so threatened by a strong, independent woman they had to make her into a bad one? An interesting analogy to Audrey Fish is never made by the student, who, thank God, has no idea who Mary Magdalene is.

PSYCHOLOGY 104: The Don't Ask Don't Tell Theory of Parenthood

Taught by Professor Daddy Lumpkin, this once popular but controversial course has been expunged from memory.

JUSTICE 101

Canceled.

HISTORY OF MODERN SLAVERY

The only course taught by the student, this trenchant recitation of heart-rending wrongs done to said student has been dropped from the syllabus.

DID YOU KNOW? On the island of Tristan da Cunha, it is illegal to teach your child Intermediate Calculus!

CAMPUS LIFE

CAMPUS

THE LECTURE
AD NAUSEAM HALL

OVERVIEW

THE BOTANICAL GARDENS

STATE-OF-THE-ART
FITNESS CENTER

SCIENCE LABORATORY/
CAFETERIA

FORMER KITCHEN:
HANDS-ON LAB IN TABLE-SETTING
AND CHEWING WITH MOUTH CLOSED

THE HERMAN & DEBBIE SCHUYLER
LUMPKIN MEMORIAL POOL

SCENIC WALK & ROUTE TO
GARBAGE CANS

THE MUSIC ROOM

THE PLEASE-
DO-NOT-TOUCH MUSEUM

ATHLETICS

CALCULUS COMPETITION

DIVISION 1 GUTTER CLEANING

THE LUMPKIN IDITAROD

BOYS CAN VACUUM, TOO!

TRACK TEAM: THE LUMPKIN LUMPS

INTRAMURAL LEAF RAKING

"MOTHER MAY I" VARSITY TEAM

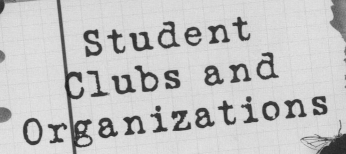

Student Clubs and Organizations

O········· **Arts and Culture**

THE DEBATE SOCIETY

Resolved: Torture is necessary to maintain homeland security.

I am living with Kim Jong-il.

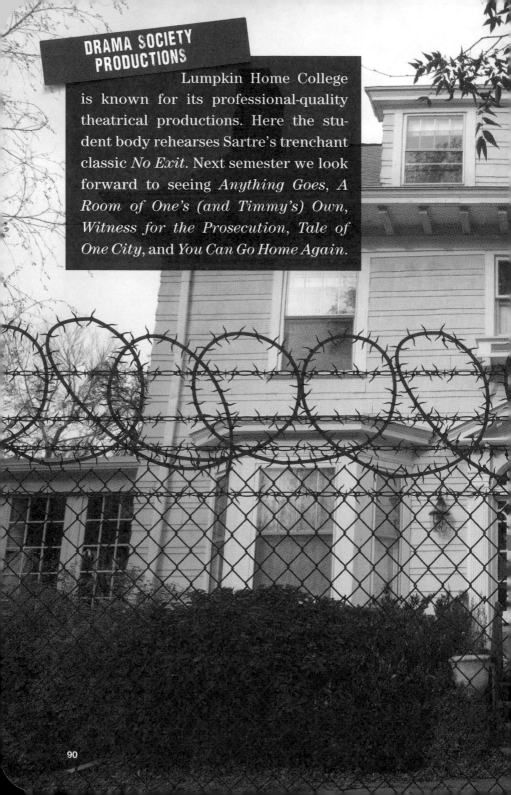

Lumpkin Home College is known for its professional-quality theatrical productions. Here the student body rehearses Sartre's trenchant classic *No Exit*. Next semester we look forward to seeing *Anything Goes*, *A Room of One's (and Timmy's) Own*, *Witness for the Prosecution*, *Tale of One City*, and *You Can Go Home Again*.

THE BIG BROTHER CLUB

A mandatory volunteer program in which student mentors and babysits Timmy for credit.

THE NATURE
CLUB

LUMPKIN
SNOW PATROL

THE CAROLING
CLUB

Fa-la-la-
la-la-la-la-
la-la

LIBERTARIANS AGAINST CURFEWS

THE FUTURE UNEMPLOYED OF AMERICA CLUB

THE HONOR SOCIETY

Note: Amnesty International does not have a branch at the college because we don't believe in amnesty.

VARSITY TOSSING BALLS OF CRUMPLED PAPER INTO THE TRASH CAN TEAM

3-point shot

HABITAT FOR HUMANITY
WITHOUT STUDENTS

Meets over Spring Break when student body goes to visit his grandmother in New Jersey.

Housing and Dining

O · · · · · · · · **Residential Life**

Decorating Your Room

Your dorm room should
reveal a personal side.
Introduce pops of color!
Pile on the pillows! And
make sure you draw a
cheerful, textured imaginary
line between your space and
Timmy's.

O ⋯⋯⋯ Defenestration Policy

Lumpkin Home College maintains a zero-tolerance
position with regards to jumping out of your window.
There is a reason that your door is locked after 9 p.m.,
and we have gone over this with both you and Audrey
Fish, as well as Mr. and Mrs. Fish.

O ⋯⋯⋯ Off-Campus Housing

One hundred percent of all Lumpkin undergraduates
live on campus.

O ⋯⋯⋯ School Menus

Subject to change without notice.

GLOBAL LUMPKIN

Offering a Junior Meal Abroad

Rules and Regulations

O ········ **Honor Code**

Enforced by video monitors and electronic ankle bracelets (see Forensic Science Center).

THE ONLY
COLLEGE IN
AMERICA
WITH A
DRESS CODE!

Dress Code

CLOTHES ↓ **MANDATORY!**

Academic Life

- - - - - - - - - - - - - -

THE CREDIT SYSTEM

GETTING OUT OF BED BEFORE 3 P.M.
.... 3 CREDITS

SHOWERING ....1 CREDIT

SHOWERING WITH SOAP ....2 CREDITS

NOT PUTTING THE
HAIRDRYER IN THE BATHTUB
WHEN SOMEONE IS TAKING
A BATH............3 CREDITS

REMEMBERING
MOTHER'S DAY....4 CREDITS

BRINGING A
MUG OF COFFEE
TO PRESIDENT
MRS. LUMPKIN
ON SUNDAY
MORNING...6 CREDITS

Graduation Speech by President Mrs. Lumpkin

Welcome Student, Parent, Brother, and Houseguest to Lumpkin Home College's first graduation.

And what a joyous day it is. So much has transpired since Bradley H. Lumpkin took not just the road less traveled, but no road at all. Others took the highway, but you, Bradley, wrecked the car in the driveway.

On a personal note, it has only been a week since the college was established and we began our remarkable journey together down these hallowed halls, but those who have recently joined our journey—the carpenter, painter, and exterminator who inspected the upstairs hallway yesterday—say they can't believe that so much damage could have been caused in a week. Congratulations, Bradley.

You know, the experts say that home colleges don't work. That we are not educating, but enabling our student body to operate a numbers game from home and open new mayonnaise jars when there are three in the fridge already open.

But guess what? I am pleased to share with you some wonderful news: One hundred percent of our student body found jobs this year! With Uncle Doug. Last month, Uncle Doug sold his condo, and now he must vacate the premises immediately. As some of you who took the Thursday night class in Trash Day Preparation know, getting rid of garbage is a very important life skill, especially when it involves a Dumpster. After four interviews with Uncle Doug, Bradley was hired. And keep your fingers crossed. If Uncle Doug's mortgage comes through, he might need someone to assemble particle-board shelves, and who better than someone who took IKEA 302?

Bradley, as you venture out into the real world, let me offer you three pieces of advice: First, do *not* follow your passion. Remember what happened last week? Second, if you think you can, you definitely cannot. Again, remember last week. Finally, don't forget that Daddy needs you to pick him up after his gum surgery at 3 o'clock Thursday, not at the main entrance but at the place where Gramz's ex got the new knee on someone else's insurance.

So, go forth, student! For you it is a happy beginning, and for us, thank God, it is a happy end and a chance to clear your things out of the rumpus room and have a sewing room.

Lumpkin Ho

LUM
HOME
MALAE CAUS

Be it known that we

Bradley H.

neither burned down the

a felony for a week and is

Dip

GOOD JOB
GOOD JOB

in honor of outstanding

Mommy
_____
President

me College

KIN
LEGE
OPTIMUM

hereby certify that

Lumpkin

house nor committed
therefore awarded this

loma

accomplishment and fortitude.

**EDUCATION
IS POWER**

Daddy

Comptroller

Leaving Lumpkin Home College

Regulation 5A mandates that graduating seniors must evacuate the premises no later than one hour after the graduation ceremony. Any student leaving behind evidence of his existence will be fined usuriously. Good luck! The world is your oyster.

ABOUT THE AUTHORS

PATRICIA MARX AND SARAH PAYNE STUART are the coauthors of *How to Regain Your Virginity* and alumnae of *The Harvard Lampoon*.

Patricia Marx, a staff writer for *The New Yorker* and a former writer for *Saturday Night Live*, is the author of the novels *Starting from Happy* and *Him, Her, Him Again, the End of Him.* She lives in New York.

Sarah Payne Stuart is the author of the novels *Men in Trouble* and *The Year Roger Wasn't Well*, and the memoirs *My First Cousin Once Removed* and, most recently, *Perfectly Miserable: Guilt, God and Real Estate in a Small Town*. She lives in Maine or New York, she isn't sure.

EXTRA CREDIT As usual, we are indebted to our roommates, Paul Roossin and Charlie Stuart. We'd also like to thank our learned professors, Suzanne Rafer, Erin Klabunde, Lisa Hollander, Anne Kerman, Michael DiMascio, James Williamson, Beth Levy, Barbara Peragine, Julie Primavera, and especially provost and thesis adviser Bruce Tracy. If we told you how much funnier they made this book, we'd get expelled for cheating.

PATRICIA MARX AND SARAH PAYNE STUART,
CLASS OF 2014

ORIGINAL PHOTOGRAPHY: Evan Sklar, Wardrobe Styling by Ellen Silverstein: front and back cover, pp. i, 1, 2 (house), 7, 8, 9, 11, 12–13, 21, 22 (bottom), 30 (Sarge), 31, 33 (Bradley), 34, 35, 36, 37, 39 (top), 40 (Sarge), 43 (holiday card), 47, 49 (Bradley) 51, (Bradley), 53 (bottom), 54, 55 (bottom), 58 (Sarge), 62, 64, 66 (Bradley), 69 (bottom), 72, 73, 75, 76, 77, 80, 81, 82, 83, 84 (top), 85, 86 (Iditarod), 87 (track team and Bradley), 88, 89, 90–91, 92, 93 (bottom), 96–97, 98–99, 101, 103 (car), 104, 108–109, 110, 113, 116–117, 118–119, 120 (house).

Special thanks to Carla Nager, Zack Willis, Elliot Mayer, Noah Gomberg, the Gomberg family, and of course, Balthazar.

ADDITIONAL STOCK PHOTOGRAPHY: age fotostock: p. 28 (mummy). **Alamy Images:** Vincent O'Byrne–p. 5(books). **Corbis:** Rick Friedman–p. 3. Michael DiMascio: pp. 26 (Audrey), 50 (Audrey), 84 (bottom), 94–95 (bottom). **Fotolia:** anankkml–p. 67; antiqueimages–p. 29 (printing press); Anyka–p. 58 (turtle); Matthew Benoit–p. 60; Bill–p. 79 (TV dinner); bloomua–p. 50; eurobanks–pp. 24–25 (chalkboard), 106–107; Zakharov Evgeniy–p. 30 (frames); Faysal Farhan–p. 4 (beer); lloyd fudge–p. 101 (pillow, top); Gajus–p. 57; goodluz–p. 6; joloei–p. 5 (laundry); kanate–p. 115 (crumpled paper); karam miri–p. 101 (pillow, bottom); kmiragaya–p. 28 (vase); Kurhan–p. 25 (bottom); Robert Mizerek–p. 26 (criminal records); Pekchar–p. 115 ("like" icon); Picture Partners–p. 81 (plants, right and left); ra2studio–p. 44; schankz–p. 95 (chairs); Dmitriy Syechin–p. 81 (plant, middle); tiero–p. 40 (delivery man); Marco Varrone–p. 49 (abacus); villorejo–p. 29 (telegraph); Guido Vrola–p. 101 (painting); willim87–p. 87 (crowd); Maksym Yemelyanov–p. 58 (scale); Feng Yu–pp. 4–5 (pizza); yuliaglam–p. 115 (seal); zorandim75–p. 43 (turtle). **Getty Images:** Daniel Allen–p. 71; David Aschkenas–p. 102; Steve Bronstein–p. 59; C Squared Studios–p. 56 (fridge); Robert Churchill–p. 4 (car); Michael Courtney–p. 81 (garage interior); Chris Craymer–p. 52; CSA Images/B&W Mex Ink Collection–p. 22 (phone); Culture Club–p. 70 (bottom); azgAr Donmaz–p. 25 (middle); Chris Fertnig–p. 66 (pew); FMB Photo–p. 2 (background); Tom Fullum–p. 25 (top); Stacy Gold–p. 86 (top, right); Daniel Grill–p. 86 (top, left); Dennis Hallinan–p. 68; Philip Lee Harvey–p. 105; Hiroshi Higuchi–p. 66 (windows); Hulton Archive/Stringer–p. 23 (both), 61; Image Source–p. 48; John Kobal Foundation–p. 22 (top, left); Mike Kemp/Rubberball–p. 69 (ice cream); Dorling Kindersley–p. 28 (slab); Jim Kruger–p. 63; Niels Laan–p. 87 (top, right); Laurie and Charles–p. 65; Peter Mason–p. 70 (top); Lane Oatey/Blue Jean Images–p. 29 (top, right); Omikron Omikron–p. 55 (top); Dimitri Otis–p. 49 (vase); Daniele Pellegrini–p. 28 (cave painting); Photodisc–p. 84 (top, right); Lauri Rotko–p. 78 (right); Zubin Shroff–p. 41 (top); Carl Smith–p. 66 (woman's head); Stockbyte–p. 4 (cash); ThomasVogel–p. 78–79 (clothesline); Tobias Tooga–p. 74; Frances Twitty–p. 51 (courtroom); Underwood Archives–pp. 78 (left); Adrian Weinbrecht–p. 41 (bottom); Andy Whale–p. 38; Woods Wheatcroft–p. 87 (wheelbarrow). **Istockphoto:** lammerst333–p. 93 (shoveling). **Masterfile:** p. 42. **Photofest:** Columbia Pictures–p. 94 (top). **SuperStock:** Classicstock.com–pp. 22 (cop), 53 (counting).